BOYS & GIRLS
ON
OLDE CAPE COD

Authentic Tales of Yesteryear's Children . . .
. . . For Today's Children

by
MARION RAWSON VUILLEUMIER

Illustrations by Louis Vuilleumier

Cover Illustration by Sheila Brown

The Butterworth Company
23 Traders Lane
West Yarmouth, Massachusetts 02673

Copyright 1968
by Marion Vuilleumier

Third Printing
1973

Revised
1980

Printed in United States

Dedicated to the

Children of Cape Cod

ACKNOWLEDGMENTS:

Appreciation is expressed to the Tales of Cape Cod, Inc., a Capewide historical organization which published the first three editions of this book to perpetuate tales of Cape Cod life for children.

FOREWORD

These stories are based on authentic incidents in the lives of children of early Cape Cod days. In some cases the children depicted here are part of history. James Jarves, John Billington, Margery Baxter, John Fulcher, Joshua Taylor and Daniel Hallett actually lived and are in written records. Sometimes historical incidents pertaining to children are mentioned but no names given. Children with Cape Cod names were then invented to illustrate these stories. This book is not intended as a text. Rather it was written to portray authentically early Cape Cod days for the children of today.

Marion Rawson Vuilleumier
West Hyannisport
Massachusetts

CONTENTS

BOY WITH A DREAM

Late one rainy night in Hyannis Daniel Hallett was awakened by a loud pounding at the door. Pilot barked wildly. Daniel crawled out of bed and looked down from the loft. Rain slashed at the windows and the wind howled. Daniel's father flung open the door. The sea dashed spray on the rocks. Men in oilskins called Daniel's father to follow.

"There's a ship sinking," they called. "Help man the lifeboat."

Father pulled on his rain gear as he rushed out the door.

"Can I come too, Father?" called Daniel.

"Daniel Bunker Hallett," said his mother, "there's not much a ten-year-old boy can do except get soaking wet. We'll wait where it's warm and dry."

She poked at the fire and filled the coffee pot, then drew Daniel in bed with her.

At dawn Daniel's father returned. Gratefully sipping his hot coffee he told the news.

"We saved every man on that ship before it went down, but the cargo is lost. There should be a range light to guide ships into our harbor."

"Why isn't there?" asked Daniel.

"The town can't afford to build a lighthouse and pay a keeper to keep a light going," said Father. His fist crashed on the table. "Something must be done though. Hyannis Harbor is dangerous."

Mother poured more coffee into Father's cup.

1

"They talk every year at town meeting about building a lighthouse," she said. "They'd better do more than talk or none of the ships will stop here anymore."

Father agreed.

"We've got to find a way to have a safe port. The Cape needs the fish, coal and lumber the ships bring."

The spring days slipped by into summer. School was out. Daniel had time to play on the beach. His favorite game was to pretend he was a lighthouse keeper. Daniel imagined himself polishing a great light so it would shine clearly. He picked the perfect place for the lighthouse out on the rocky point.

Daniel would lie on the warm sand day dreaming about the ships from other countries that would sail by his light. What would they look like? Then Pilot would find a butterfly or a crab and bark furiously. Daniel would come to with a start, only a little boy with a great big dream.

One morning when Daniel sat down to breakfast, his father had news of another ship that had barely missed the treacherous shoals.

"Daniel," he said, "let's build a light on the point ourselves. You are old enough to help. Between us we could keep the light going. It would be better than no light at all."

"Sure, Dad," said Daniel eagerly. "Can we start this morning?"

Pilot barked and raced around the house until Daniel's mother put him out.

"We'll start right away," said his father. "I figure that between us we can man a light every night through the summer."

It took Daniel's father and his men three days to fix a make-shift lighthouse. They moved an old cranberry shed down to the rocky point, then built bunks, chairs and a table. Out of the loft they constructed a tower with open sides. Daniel's father bought the largest lantern he could find and hung it in the tower. A large mirror was placed behind the light.

"The mirror will reflect the light far out over the water," explained Daniel's father. Finally a large barrel of whale oil was brought in.

"Being a lighthouse keeper is going to be fun," said Daniel as he hurried along by his father. "Mother will miss us at home tonight though."

Pilot sensed the adventure and raced around them in circles.

"She doesn't mind," said Father, "for she knows we might save a ship."

First Daniel and his father made the beds, then they ate supper from the basket Mother had prepared. Next Daniel learned how to light and shut off the lantern. Finally the lantern was again lighted and hung under the pointed roof. The polished mirror reflected light that dazzled Daniel's eyes.

Daniel climbed down from the loft and sat outside to watch for ships. There were none that night but there was a beautiful sunset.

Pilot turned out to be a natural lighthouse keeper's dog, for at dawn he woke them with his barking as if to tell them it was time to put out the light. Then it was time to walk back home for Mother's hot breakfast.

After that Daniel and his father took turns staying with the light throughout the summer. Daniel stayed most of the time, because his father had cranberry bogs to care for and a fishing business to run. That summer there were no wrecks. In the fall Daniel manned the lighthouse for awhile, walking home early for a warm breakfast before he walked to school.

When the cold weather came they could no longer stay with the light. There was no heat and school was getting harder. Daniel and his father continued to man the light the following summers.

One early spring evening a Town Selectman stopped by. Daniel laid aside his school books and listened.

"We appreciate the light you and your son have kept going these past few summers," the Selectman said. "The town treasury is in pretty good shape this year. We think we can ask town meeting to vote a lighthouse." The Selectman looked at Daniel's father.

"If we build a lighthouse will you be the keeper? We can probably pay enough so you won't have to do all your other jobs."

Daniel's father smiled, noticing the happy grin on Daniel's face.

"We'll be proud to keep the harbor light for the town," Father said. "I'll move my family in as soon as it is built."

"Great!" exclaimed Daniel as he reached out to quiet Pilot. "I've always wanted to live in a real lighthouse."

Daniel eventually became a banker in Boston. Often he returned to Cape Cod to visit. Looking across the water to the range light, which now was automatic, he would often say, "I like being a banker, but I'll never forget the thrill of my first job, lighting the new light when I was assistant lighthouse keeper."

GOVERNOR BRADFORD MAKES A FRIEND

In the year 1627, Laughing Water lay ill in her home on the bank of the Manomet River. The usually happy little Indian girl was quiet and listless. Her feverish body was full of pain. Her father, Sachem Cawnacome, watched anxiously.

"I do not understand why your herbs do not make her better," he said, turning to Laughing Water's mother.

Nearby at the new Aptuxcet Trading Post, Isaac and Edward, two servants of the Plymouth Colony, were working in their garden.

"I've never seen a little girl so ill," said Isaac, leaning on his hoe. "She hardly knew me when I stopped by this morning. Sachem Cawnacome and his family are such good friends. I wish we could do something to help them now."

"Remember how he helped us five years ago during that famine?" said Edward. "We were so hungry at Plymouth and Sachem Cawnacome sold Governor Bradford some corn and beans. Nothing ever tasted better."

The men started hoeing again, but rather slowly.

"I wonder why the Sachem would never visit Plymouth. Governor Bradford asked him many times. I think Laughing Water would like the Pilgrim children," said Isaac.

"Maybe he is afraid to go among so many strange people," said Edward.

"I don't see why he should be," said Isaac, starting another row. "We've always been good friends."

Isaac stopped and looked out over the Manomet River and beyond where it entered Great Bay. "Cawnacome helped us pick the best place for this Trading Post."

Then he cried out and pointed. "Look, Edward, a sail! It must be the Dutch Trader's ship."

"Let's finish the chores," said Edward, "so we can go to the ship when it anchors. I'll feed the pigs." He leaned his hoe against the Trading Post and picked up a bucket.

Later that afternoon the sound of trumpets came faintly across the water. The ship was anchoring in the Bay. The Dutch trader de Rasiere had arrived from New Amsterdam (New York). Isaac and Edward stepped into their shallop and eagerly rowed toward the large ship. Travelers seldom came to the trading post.

"I hope there will be some letters for us," said Isaac. "I wonder what news we'll hear."

"I hope there will be a doctor on board who can help Laughing Water," puffed Edward.

Mr. de Rasiere came on deck to greet Isaac and Edward.

"Please guide me right away to Governor Bradford at New Plymouth," said he. "I am not anxious to walk twenty miles over land, so we'll carry the shallop to Scussett River and go by water."

"Yes, sir," said Isaac. "But first, do you have a doctor on board? Our Sachem's daughter is very sick. She has a strange fever."

"No," said de Rasiere. "No doctor came with us and I have no medicine."

"We'll get an early start to New Plymouth tomorrow morning then," said Isaac. "Maybe we can bring back help from there."

Mr. de Rasiere was ready early the next day. Isaac, Edward and some of the trader's men rowed up the Manomet River as far as they could. When the waters became narrow and shallow, they emptied the light weight shallop and carried it on their shoulders for six miles through the woods until they reached the beginnings of the Scusset River.

"Captain Standish says some day there should be a canal here," said Isaac.

"That would be fine," replied de Rasiere. "Ships could avoid the dangerous shoals off Cape Cod. It would save much time."

Soon the shallop was back in the water and the men rowed down the river and across the bay to New Plymouth.

Several days later voices rang through the woods near the Aptuxcet Trading Post as a large party approached from New Plymouth. Governor Bradford was there, chatting with his friend de Rasiere. Many men of Plymouth had come to exchange their furs for sugar, linen and tobacco that de Rasiere had on his bark.

Isaac and Edward did not have trading on their minds then. They were thinking of Laughing Water, and went immediately to her home. She was no better.

"Give her this," said Isaac to Laughing Water's mother. "There is a fever which bothers the Indians now that the White men have come. For this we are very sorry. This powder just came from England and it has cured fevers in Plymouth. Maybe it will help your daughter."

Laughing Water's parents looked anxiously at each other. Should they try the white man's medicine? Would it hurt or help their little girl?

Cawnacome said, "Let us try it. The men from New Plymouth have never done us any harm."

Laughing Water's mother roused the girl and gave her the medicine. She swallowed it all and sank back into a light sleep. Her worried parents sat by her side, watching through the night. By morning Laughing Water was better. Her fever was down and she ate some food for the first time in days.

Laughing Water was weak but smiling when Governor Bradford stopped to see his old friend. In Bradford's hand was a small knife with a carved bone handle.

"It is for you, Laughing Water," he said. "This came from the Dutch ship. When you are well again will you and your father visit us in Plymouth?"

"We will come," said Cawnacome. "Thank you for bringing life back to my little daughter."

WHEN THE HERRING RAN

One May day Sally sat on the bank below the Brewster mill watching the herring squirming and leaping to get upstream. The water glittered with silver as the sun shone on the glistening fish.

"What makes them try so desperately to swim upstream?" she wondered.

Every spring since she could remember the herring fought to leave the ocean and push high up the streams on the Cape. Always up, up, up they had to go.

One big fellow jumped higher than the rest. Sally's empty lunch pail tipped over as she scrambled along the banking to follow him upstream. She leaped from stone to stone in the shallow water watching the fish's silvery body twist and leap upwards.

"I wonder if he can get over the dam beside the mill," she thought, as she ran around the edge of the mill pool.

Sally knelt at the edge of the dam and looked over. There was the big fellow leaping higher and higher, but not quite high enough.

"If only the town had built the passageway beside the dam for the herring," Sally mused. "Father says there will soon be a herring run now that Mr. Gray was made regulator of the herring brook, but it won't be in time for Big Fellow." She watched the leaping fish.

With a last desperate effort he flopped over the dam and started upstream again. He left a pool full of fish. The water seemed alive there were so many moving herring in it.

Two men were at the bank across from Sally.

"Father," she squealed, as she jumped up and raced back below the pool to cross the stream. The men carried barrels and nets. "May I net some herring", she asked, arriving a little breathless.

"Good idea," said Father. "Together we'll fill the barrel sooner." Sally dipped the net into the pond and pulled it up full of wiggling fish. Her father helped her empty the net into the barrel.

"Let's fill another barrel," she said when the first was filled to the top.

"Not while I'm around," laughed Mr. Gray. "Only one barrel to a family this week. You can get more after a few days."

"That rule is made so everyone can have his share," explained Sally's father. "Don't worry. We'll have plenty to eat and enough to salt away for the winter, too. The herring will run awhile yet."

Sally picked up her pail and followed her father home. A delicious smell greeted them at the door.

"Wash up for supper," called Mother. "The herring is almost ready."

Sally paused a minute to watch her mother dip the fish into cornmeal and place them in a frying pan.

"Where do the herring come from?" asked Sally at the supper table.

"They swim all over the ocean," answered her mother. "These could have come from off the coast of England or maybe even up as far as Sweden or Norway."

"They never forget where they are born and in the spring they turn toward Cape Cod," added her father.

"Why do they try so hard to get upstream?" asked Sally, passing her plate for more fish.

"They want to reach the quiet places in the upper

stream and lay eggs to spawn new herring," said Mother.

Sally chewed her fish, wondering if her mouthful had been near Ireland or maybe Scotland.

"Their travels are as mysterious as their name," added Father. "I never could see why herring are called alewives."

Suddenly Sally choked. A herring bone was stuck in her throat. Mother slapped her hard on the back. Sally coughed and choked again. The bone did not move. She could hardly breath. How her throat hurt!

"Run for Dr. Forbes," cried Sally's mother as she tipped Sally over her chair. Father raced out the door. Sally was thankful the doctor lived just up the path.

A few minutes later Dr. Forbes came in, puffing and panting. Out came the forceps from his bag. Sally shut her eyes and opened her mouth wide. A gurgle, a choke, a sharp pain, and the bone was out. She could barely gasp out her thanks.

"You're a brave girl," said the doctor. "This is the tenth bone I've taken out in the last few days. I always know when the herring start to run even if I don't go by the brook."

"I think I'll keep the bone," said Sally, looking at it in her hand. "It will remind me of the fish who travel all over the ocean."

"I hope it will remind you to chew more carefully when you eat herring," said her mother.

THE BOY WHO MADE AN ISLAND

One clear day in late summer, Joshua and his dog Brownie ran along the sand after a flock of sheep. The sun was bright, making the sand warm under the boy's bare feet.

Although Joshua kept his eyes mostly on the sheep, he sent quick glances each side of the sandy path. His father depended on him each day to bring the flock to the fine grazing land which lay on a high point of land beyond the sandy dunes, but Joshua was also looking for beach plums for his mother. She made jelly from the fruit and sold it to the summer tourists. Joshua helped her by gathering the plums.

Big Sam, the leader of the flock, was plodding along at the head. The sheep were dutifully following him, while Brownie trotted along in the rear. Since everything was all right with the flock, Joshua began looking to the left for a large clump of beach plum bushes he remembered seeing before. There they were! Joshua darted off the path to the waist high bushes and felt of the fruit. The little round plums were hard and still not ready to leave the bush. They would not be ready for another day or two.

Joshua was so busy with the plums, he had forgotten the sheep. They were out of sight. Brownie's barking told him something was wrong. The boy raced back to the path and over the dunes. Soon he saw Big Sam off to the left. The sheep had left the path and was munching in a big patch of thick grass. The other sheep had also taken the wrong turn, plodding after their leader, in spite of Brownie's furious barks.

Joshua finally reached Big Sam and tried to start him back toward the main path. Big Sam wouldn't budge. He planted his four feet firmly and munched on. He didn't want to leave his tasty lunch. Joshua got behind him and pushed hard, while Brownie nipped at the animal's heels. Finally Big Sam gave in. Bleating in protest he walked unwillingly back to the path. The rest of the flock trailed along behind him.

After this Joshua didn't leave the flock again. It was low tide and the sheep might easily stray before they reached their grazing grounds. Carefully Joshua brought them through the sandy dunes and out to the point. This was a high headland at the end of a sandy strip. Here the grass was green and thick. Now all Joshua had to do was stay near the sandy strip that connected the point with the mainland. It was the only way off.

Big Sam and his flock started lunching happily on the grasses. Joshua and Brownie lunched happily too. They had food from the basket Joshua's mother had packed. Brownie settled down to watch the sheep while Joshua searched for beach plums. Most of them were not ready, but he did collect enough to fill his basket.

Now Joshua was sleepy. The animals were already dozing, and Joshua lay down to rest. Later, when the sun started going down, the breeze became cool. This awakened the boy, who yawned and stretched. He called Brownie and together they started the sheep homeward. The flock went quickly, thinking perhaps of the supper which awaited them in their shed. Joshua had to walk rapidly to keep up with them.

They traveled down across the dunes. The tide was high now and the way was narrow. The boy loved the place about half way across where at high tide the dunes dipped almost to the sea. Joshua imagined the hungry ocean was trying to climb across the sandy strip and make a channel. Just for fun, Joshua made a line with his toe where he imagined the sea wanted to go. The little trough extended a long way when it finally touched the water on both sides. The boy was fascinated and dug along the trench again, this time with his heel. He watched as the sea water flowed along the trough like a little river.

Suddenly the boy noticed that the sun had gone and wisps of fog were forming. Also, the sheep had trudged out of sight. Joshua ran to catch up to the animals, sighing thankfully when he saw them ahead on the right path. The fog was closing in fast and he urged them on. They arrived home just as it was getting so thick Joshua could hardly see the whole flock.

That night the sea became angry. It curled and snarled up all over the shores of the Cape. A northeast storm had blown up. The next day and the next Joshua and Brownie couldn't go out to the point. The rain and the wind would have drenched them. Joshua's father said it was the worst storm he had seen. Finally the northeaster blew itself out to sea and a new day dawned sunny and warm.

Joshua set out with his lunch, his dog and the sheep for the grazing grounds. As he came up the first high dune and looked across the grassy headland, he gasped. Some of the dunes had disappeared. Joshua's little trough had become a channel. The grassy point was now an island. Joshua's big toe had given the sea the start it needed to reach across the dunes. Now the boy couldn't take his sheep to their grazing grounds. He turned the flock around and started home with the news, feeling badly that the sheep could no longer enjoy the thick grass on the point.

The following summer Joshua's father said, "I think Big Sam and the flock can still graze on the point. Today you can help me build a barge, Joshua."

Joshua pounded nails and fetched wood, helping his father build a large raft. When it was finished, they rolled the barge on logs down into the water and anchored it for the night. The next day Joshua and Brownie helped herd the sheep toward the gangplank. The animals bleated nervously and stamped their hooves at this new experience.

"Nip at Big Sam," Joshua called to Brownie. "If he'll go the others will follow."

Brownie barked, Joshua pushed and Father called. Reluctantly Big Sam moved forward. Soon the flock was on the barge and sailing down the channel toward the island. It was easier getting the flock off. The luscious green grass ahead made Big Sam hurry.

The sheep grazed happily on the island during the warm summer days and nights, while Joshua went fishing with his father, gathered beach plums for his mother and sold jelly at the front yard stand. The sheep grew fat as their wool coats thickened, grazing safely on the old point now that it was an island.

GRANDPA AND THE WINDMILL

Henry Hall was awakened early one morning by a loud creaking sound. The boy jumped out of bed and ran to the window. The arms of Grandfather's huge windmill next door were turning furiously. The wind bent the small pines and pushed against the windmill. The mill creaked and groaned. Henry had never seen the arms go round so fast.

The boy turned and dressed quickly. Grandpa was going to have a job to grind corn today. The wind was about as strong as the hurricane his father often told him about. As Henry went down the stairs to breakfast, he remembered the old verse about the Baxter Boys' Mill in Yarmouth. His feet kept time down the stair treads with the rhyme:

> The Baxter boys they built a mill,
> Sometimes it went, sometimes stood still,
> And when it went it made no noise
> Because it was built by the Baxter Boys.

"Even the Baxter boys' mill would make a noise today," thought Henry.

After finishing his cornmeal and drinking his milk, Henry picked up his school books and walked to the mill to see his Grandpa Henry Hall. Grandpa was an important man in town and Henry was glad he was named for him.

Grandpa Henry was inside, pouring corn into the trough that ran between the two mill stones. Soon the corn would come out ground fine into the cornmeal Henry loved Grandpa anxiously watched the whirling mill stones.

"I'll have to climb up the arms again, Henry, and take in more sail. This is a tarnation hard wind," Grandpa said. "I don't like to do it in this wind, but these stones are going too fast."

Grandpa and Henry went outside and looked up at the four arms and the sails that were fastened part way up each one.

"Lucky you were once a sailor," said Henry. Grandpa climbed the arms as if they were ships masts. When the wind was strong he had to shorten sail on each arm. Other times he had to unfurl the sail to catch every breeze.

"You run along, boy," said Grandpa, "or you'll be late for school. You can't watch me climb this morning."

Slowly Henry started on his three-mile walk. There wouldn't be anything as exciting as this at school.

The wind blew worse as Henry studied. His teacher kept looking out the window.

"It's the hardest blow anyone can remember," he said. "You children go straight home when school is over."

At last school was out and Henry was free to run home. He raced all the way, leaning into the strong wind.

Soon Henry could see the windmill. Its arms were still turning wildly but the sails were furled. Grandpa was still up there! Henry could see his red shirt behind the arms. Hooray! He could see Grandpa do his sailing tricks.

Then Henry looked again. Something was wrong. The great chain that held the windmill still when Grandpa was aloft was swinging loose. The mill arms weren't the only thing turning. The mill itself was circling round and round. Grandpa couldn't get down. He was straddling the turning shaft on which the arms were fastened. Grandpa had to keep lifting himself off the shaft each time it turned so he wouldn't be thrown to the ground.

Henry ran faster than ever in his life. If Grandpa fell he would be badly hurt. Running into his house he shouted as loud as he could. Mother came running. Father was just coming up the road and he rushed to help. The three of them caught the anchor chain and brought the mill to a stop.

Grandpa climbed down slowly, his arms and legs shaking.

"Henry," he said when he could catch his breath, "I'm sure glad you love windmills and came straight home today."

"I'm glad you were a sailor so you could stay up there when the windmill got loose," said Henry.

The boy was quiet the rest of the afternoon. By supper time the wind was dying down and he had a new rhyme. "It is as good as the one about the Baxter Boys," thought Henry.

> "Grandpa Henry built a mill,
>   Sometimes it went, sometimes stood still.
> Because he once a ship did sail
>   He rode a windmill in a gale."

A BEACH COMBER'S TREASURE

The threatening thunder in the sky and the mountainous waves of the ocean frightened 10-year-old John Fulcher, cabin boy of the ship "Wave", as he looked out of the galley port hole.

The captain strode by on his way to the wheelhouse. His face looked worried, for the ship's glass was sinking fast. The first mate hurried by on his way below to call more crew men to haul in the sail. "It's the worst blow yet," John heard him mutter.

Then the mate raised his voice, "All hands on deck!"

Dropping his kitchen knife, John sprang to help. As he reached the top of the companionway, the force of the wind almost threw him over backwards. The fast driven clouds, the huge waves and the screeching wind frightened John more. He reached for a rope. This unfriendly ocean was very different from the peaceful sea he had known on the voyage from England. This would happen, just as they were almost to America, off the Cape Cod shores!

All the seamen were furling sail rapidly, when the central mast snapped like a toothpick. The ship veered helplessly in the trough of the waves.

"It's a bad storm and its getting worse, Sonny," said the mate. "You might lose your footing. Come, I'll lash you to what's left of this mast."

The mate's kindly voice was the last John heard from any crewmen, for all were busy hanging on to stay alive.

Shortly after, the ship lurched again as the second mast broke. Darkness came and John bobbed up and down on the deck. Wave after wave dashed over him. He remembered nothing more of the storm after the ship, with an enormous crash, hit the shoals.

John was awakened with the surf pounding in his ears. It was daylight. He was still lashed to the mast which had come to rest on the sand bar near shore. Bits of wood were all around him but not a living thing was in sight.

John lay helpless, terror stricken, dreading the pounding of the returning tide. How could he get out of reach of the icy waters which might toss him back into the sea?

About a mile away, Freeman Mayo was tramping Nauset Beach looking for wood, cargo or anything floating in on the tide. He always went beach combing after a big storm. Nauset was on the treacherous backside of the Cape, where many ships were wrecked. In the past Mr. Mayo had found ship's paneling for his living room, rope for fishing and a keg of nails for building. He was sorry for people who perished in the wrecks but he was grateful for any of the debris that came his way. What would he find today?

Mr. Mayo strode over the dunes, watching the boiling surf carefully. He saw a large piece of wreckage on a sandbar near shore. Looking closer, he dashed forward. That looked like a person lashed to a broken mast, right in the path of the incoming tide. As he splashed into the water he was amazed to see that it was a young boy.

"Lad, lad, what a fix you are in!" Mr. Mayo cried. Rapidly he cut the ropes and released John. The boy was numb from the cold and the ropes. He could not stand. Mr. Mayo wrapped him in his own coat and carried him home.

"Here is a beach comber's treasure," Mr. Mayo called as he carried John through the door. Immediately John felt the warmth of the fireplace and the boisterous welcome of the Mayo children.

John thawed out gradually. His new friends, especially Bill and Dick Mayo who were about his own age, were spellbound as he told of the shipwreck. Then John was spellbound as he listened to the children's chatter and looked around the room, receiving his first impressions of life on Cape Cod.

For several weeks John stayed with the Mayos, regaining his strength and hoping to hear news of his shipmates from the "Wave". Finally it was clear that no one had lived through the shipwreck except John.

One evening at supper time Freeman Mayo said, "John, I've just contacted an English brig at Provincetown. The ship is setting sail for England soon, and the captain will take you on as cabin boy."

Dick let out a whoop. "Boy, would I like to go to sea! You're in luck, John".

Bill seconded the idea. "When can I be a cabin boy like you were, Father," he wheedled.

"Everyone seems anxious to go but John," observed Mr. Mayo. "Why so silent, John? Don't you want to go home?"

"No, sir," John blurted out, "I couldn't take any more of that sea. Please can I stay on Cape Cod?"

"You may indeed," answered Mr. Mayo. "We won't force a boy to go to sea against his will. Our neighbor Ezekiel Doane needs some help on his farm. We'll go see him tomorrow."

John settled down on the Doane farm. Though he was homesick for England at times, he became a contented Cape Codder. Eventually he had a wife and family of his own. He thought no more of returning to England because of the treacherous ocean that lay in between.

Years later, a Cable Station was started on the North Eastham shore. John and some neighbors went to talk with the first arrivals. He recognized some familiar accents.

"Where in England are you from?" asked John.

"Near London, Mate," said one. "Do you know it?"

"I do indeed," cried John, and launched into the story of his stormy arrival on Cape Cod.

Through the days that followed, John's new friends urged him to return with them to England for a visit.

"We'll pick a big ship, John, one that won't founder. Do come," they said.

"I will," responded John finally, making one of the biggest decisions of his life.

THE SHIRT THAT WOULD NOT DRY

Reuben strutted proudly around his yard early one summer morning showing off his new red shirt. His home was on the shore at Dennis, out of sight of any other house. Without a person anywhere in view, Reuben paraded as if he had an applauding audience. His mother had woven material on her loom, cut it out and made it into a beautiful shirt for Reuben's birthday today. He was going to take care of his new treasure.

Reuben's older brother Christopher called. The imaginary audience forgotten, Reuben raced around the house to the back where the salt vats were. The men who worked for his father were getting ready to open the gate and let ocean water gush in. Reuben and Christopher loved to watch this. It was fun to see salt made from the sea.

Reuben dashed up to Grandpa Sears and Christopher as they stood watching the men.

"Not much like the old days," said Grandpa, as he puffed on his pipe. "We used to boil sea water in big black kettles until only salt was left. That was a job, keeping the fires going until the water boiled away. Didn't get much salt either."

"Tell us about your better idea," pleaded Reuben, who loved to hear Grandpa's often told story. Grandpa hadn't much else to do these days, and he didn't need much urging to start story telling.

"When I was a youngster," he began, "I got mighty tired of feeding wood to the fires under the big pots; I'd try to figure out an easier way to get the salt. When I was grown up and had some time, I built some great shallow troughs like giant sand boxes. I let the sea into them. I figured that if the water sat long enough the sun would do the work. It did, too. When the water evaporated, salt was left."

"That first year I only got eight bushels," said Grandpa, knocking his pipe against a tree. "It was a lot better, though, than wasting all that time and wood boiling kettles of water. After that I built more troughs and got more salt. I had enough for my family and to sell, too!"

Reuben heard a rushing noise. The men had removed a board, and seawater swirled down a tiny canal from the pond above. The tall creaking windmill on the pond's edge turned its huge arms, laboring to pump more water up the hill from the sea to the salt pond Father had made. Father needed lots of water in the pond, so that he could let water into his salt vats whenever he needed to.

"Father makes lots of salt," boasted Reuben.

"Your father has the best salt works on the whole Cape," said Grandpa. "I used to think he was crazy when he ran away to sea. But when he built his salt troughs as tight as a ship, I could see his sea days weren't wasted."

"I like the way Father sends the water through lots of troughs, not just one," said Reuben, as a workman removed a board and let water from a second vat into a third.

"It makes more salt that way," agreed Grandpa.

Reuben and Christopher jumped onto the edge of the first trough. Now that there was nothing more to watch, they started teetering down the vat's rim, balancing with their arms. This was their teeter game, in which the brothers tried to walk the rims of all seven vats without falling. If they did fall, it meant a drop to the ground on one side, or a ducking on the other. Since the water was only a foot deep, it wasn't dangerous, but it was exciting.

Reuben forgot all about his new shirt and gaily teetered down the first vat. Here the rope-like plant life clung to the vat's sides and was left behind when the water flowed on to vats two and three. Slimy water was left behind on the sides and the bottom. Reuben was extra careful not to fall in here!

Next came the three pickle room vats, where the lime fell on the bottom as the water flowed to the last vat. The water stayed here a long time while the sun did its work.

When only salt crystals and bitter water were left, Father shoveled the crystals into storing sheds to dry. Bitter water was put into a trough. Epsom Salts and Glauber Salts were made from this bitter water after the weather became cold. Reuben at eight years could hardly pronounce these names, and he didn't know much about them. He did know that his family used salt crystals from the seventh vat at the table.

Christopher and Reuben inched safely by the last of the vats and jumped to the ground with a whoop. Another perfect score! Christopher ran off to help his father in the fields, while Reuben, still forgetting about his new shirt, jumped up on the bitter water vat to practice teetering.

Suddenly, before he knew how it had happened, Reuben was falling. Into the vat he plunged. He and his clothes were soaked. Then he remembered his new shirt.

"Too bad to get it wet the first day," he thought sadly. Reuben clambered out of the water and ran to the house to change his clothes.

"Lucky it's a warm day," he thought. "The shirt will dry before Mother gets home from Aunt Sarah's tonight."

Reuben didn't want his mother to know he had been so careless with her gift.

At noon, when the rest of the family came in to eat, Reuben was crying.

"What's the matter," said Grandpa.

"My new shirt won't dry," sobbed Reuben, after telling of his accident. "I hung it up three whole hours ago by the sun dial, but it hasn't dried a bit."

"Which vat did you fall into?" said Grandpa.

When Reuben pointed out the bitter water vat, Grandpa laughed and said, "I thought so. Nothing that falls in that water will dry quickly. Your father makes that for people who work on animal skins. These people want the leather to dry slowly. Water from Glauber salt helps the skins to take several months to dry. Reuben, if you left your shirt there all summer it wouldn't dry. Now wash your shirt out in water from the pump. Then hang it up and it will soon be ready to wear."

Reuben dried his tears and did as Grandpa said. He kept feeling of the cloth every few minutes. Yes. It was drying. By the time Mother's carriage turned down the lane, Reuben was putting on his new dry shirt.

SARAH'S SURPRISE

Sarah walked across the fields one September morning in Harwich on her way to the cranberry bog. The slanting rays of the sun fell on the nodding goldenrod, making a gold carpet against the blue sky. Her friend Nathan bounded across the field to join her.

"It's going to be a great day," said Nathan. "I'm glad they closed school to let us pick cranberries. I hate to be inside this weather."

"It would be a nicer day if Mother was well," said Sarah sadly.

"So she's no better," said Nathan. "I'm sorry to hear that."

"Dr. Baker can't find what is causing her low fever," answered Sarah, turning on to the dusty cart path. "She rests most of the time and she won't eat much of anything."

"That's a shame," said Nathan, swinging his lunch pail. "It's not good to have fever on a warm day like this will be. What she needs is something cool."

Then, wanting to cheer her, he asked, eyeing her blue dress and matching apron, "Say, isn't that a new dress?"

"I just finished it," said Sarah, turning around as she skipped along. "It was very hard sewing the oilcloth, though." She stopped and pointed to the blue oilcloth that covered the lower part of her apron.

"But it was worth doing. Now I won't get wet when I kneel in the damp bog." She swung her blue sunbonnet back and forth as she walked.

Soon Nathan and Sarah reached the bog and jumped across the ditch that surrounded the cranberry plants. Many other people were already at work. Mrs. Howes, who owned the bog, waved at them and pointed towards two long sections of plants marked off with string.

Sarah knelt and set down her pail. Her quick fingers pulled berries from the low vines and dropped them clinking into her pail. Nathan worked in the next section using a cranberry scoop. Sarah stopped a minute to rest and watched him. Nathan pushed the teeth of the scoop through the vines and brought up almost a cupful of berries each time. He picked out the leaves then dumped the berries into his pail. Sarah sighed. Scoops were much faster, but too heavy for her to use. She returned to her task.

Soon Nathan's large pail and Sarah's smaller one were full. They walked toward Mrs. Howes, emptied their pails into the wooden crates beside her and watched Mrs. Howes put another black mark beside their names in her book.

"Aren't you glad these aren't school black marks?" laughed Mrs. Howes. Nathan and Sarah counted the black marks by their names. These stood for the pails of berries they had picked yesterday.

"I'd never pass if I had that many at school," said Nathan.

"I'm glad to have a lot here, though," said Sarah. "I need enough money for a new best dress and bonnet. When you pay me for picking all those pails of cranberries I'll have almost enough. After today I should have enough to buy the cloth."

Nathan and Sarah walked back to their places.

"Look at the cranes!" said Sarah, pointing overhead. "My grandfather said that's how cranberries got their name. Only cranes would eat them at first."

"I'll bet those birds wish we would all go home so they could have a cranberry feast," said Nathan, kneeling down again in the bog.

The sun rose and the day grew hotter as Nathan and Sarah picked pail after pail full. Soon it was lunch time.

Sarah and Nathan joined the other pickers in the shade of the trees near the bog and pulled their lunches from their large pockets.

As Sarah ate she looked around at the green bog with reddish tint, the goldenrod in the fields beyond and the sunlight dancing on the blue sea in the distance.

"This is like the picture my mother made for our parlor wall," said the girl with a sweep of her hand. Then she added wistfully, "I hope she'll soon feel like painting again."

Nathan nodded in sympathy watching the cranes soar overhead.

When lunch was over everyone returned to the bog and set to work again. Glancing over at Sarah, Nathan saw her scowl.

"A penny for your thoughts," he said.

"I was thinking of my Great-Grandma Sarah Hall," said Sarah. "I was named for her you know."

"Why does that make you frown"? laughed Nathan curiously.

"Because I'd like to be as smart as she was and I don't know how," explained Sarah.

"What was she so smart about?" queried Nathan, resting a moment.

"She invented a recipe when she needed one," answered Sarah, berries still falling in her pail. "She made the first cranberry jelly. Now I'd like to make something new and cool out of cranberries to bring to Mother, but I can't think of anything."

31

"I remember hearing about your great-grandparents from my folks," said Nathan. "They said it was your great-grandpa Henry Hall who grew the first cranberries for sale after he made the first bog."

"Yes, and when the preacher and his wife were coming to dinner Grandma wanted to give them something different," said Sarah, who knew the story by heart. "She had just gotten some white sugar, which was new then. She put cranberries in water and boiled them with sugar. When it had cooled Grandpa Hall said it was the best relish he had ever tasted. Grandma served it to the minister and everyone wanted the recipe."

"Cranberries caught on fast," said Nathan. "There are lots of bogs on the Cape now. My father says people off the Cape want as many as we can grow."

"It's a good thing, too," said Sarah, standing up with a full pail. "I wouldn't be able to have a new dress each fall if it wasn't for cranberry picking."

"Keep on thinking," advised Nathan as they both walked toward the cranberry crates. "If your great-grandma could invent a new recipe I'm sure you can."

Sarah's fingers and thoughts flew as she started to pick again. "I wonder if I could make a cranberry pudding," she thought, recalling the different dishes her mother had taught her to make. "If I mixed cranberry juice and sugar and thickened it with Irish moss then put in whipped egg white I'd have a very light pudding."

"Nathan," she said aloud. "If I made some pudding how could I keep it cool?"

"That's easy," responded the boy. "Put it down the well."

Sarah could hardly wait for picking time to end. She hurried back home to make her surprise. Mother was resting, so Sarah had the kitchen to herself. First she quickly checked the crock to see if there was enough Irish moss left.

"Good," she said to herself. "I'm glad we gathered a lot of this seaweed the last time we went to the shore."

Everything went well except that she almost tipped over the pail of cranberry pudding as she was lowering it down the well with a rope.

Mother got up to help Sarah with supper, but she didn't eat much. Then Sarah brought out her cranberry surprise. Mother tasted the cool pudding.

"Sarah, this is delicious," she said. "It tastes cool slipping down my throat. I believe I'll have some more."

Later when Mother was again resting, Sarah walked over to Nathan's house carrying cranberry pudding for his family.

"I think Mother is a little better," she said to Nathan. "At least she ate a dishful of my cranberry surprise, which is more than she has eaten anytime this week."

"Great," said Nathan, eating his cranberry pudding with enjoyment. "Everybody will like this. Soon there will be two Sarah Halls famous for cranberry recipes."

THE HAT THAT CAUSED A SCHOOL

In the little Indian town of Mashpee, Jim walked toward the fresh water pond where he liked to fish. The March wind played tricks. It ruffled the branches of the pine tree and kicked up clouds of dust on the dirt road. It even blew down Grannie Mendes' light blanket she had hung on a blueberry bush to air.

A car came chugging up the road. Jim stopped and stared at the automobile. Who was the important looking stranger driving? Not many outsiders went through Mashpee. Jim stepped back on the grass to let the car pass.

A gust of wind lifted the stranger's hat off and rolled it across the road into a field. In a moment it would be in the cranberry bog! Jim dropped his fishing pole and ran after the hat. The wind teased him. Each time he reached for the hat the wind blew it away. Finally the hat snagged on a holly tree at the edge of the bog. Jim reached for the hat and took it back to the stranger.

The man smiled and held out his hand. In it was a shiny dime.

"Thank you, my boy, for getting my hat. Here is some money for your trouble."

Jim shook his head.

"Oh no, sir," he said. "I can't take money for getting your hat. My mother told me to help people whenever I could. She told me not to take money for doing a favor."

The stranger patted Jim's shoulder and smiled.

"Not only are you helpful, you are also polite," he said. "Sometimes the boys and girls forget good manners."

About twenty-five years later Jim and the people of Mashpee were surprised when the Selectmen received a letter from a lawyer in Boston. It said: "Mr. Samuel G. Davis of Roxbury always remembered a Mashpee boy who refused money for doing a kind deed. To show his thanks, Mr. Davis remembered the school children of Mashpee in his will. He had set aside a fund years ago and it had now grown to $50,000. It had been left to the town for a 'Kind Good Manners' fund. From this each year the sum of two hundred dollars was to be used for five and ten dollar prizes for Mashpee children who were the most polite and courteous."

Everyone in Mashpee was delighted with this news, especially Jim, who remembered rescuing the hat years ago.

In June of 1930 the people of Mashpee gathered in the tiny old school for closing exercises. The principal read the list of prizes for good manners. Everyone clapped as the winners went forward to receive their awards.

As the crowd was leaving the building, Jim heard one selectman say to another, "We have good teachers but a very old building. We need a new school like the others on Cape Cod."

"Mr. Davis left more money than we need for prizes," said the second Selectman. "Maybe we could put the extra money toward the school."

"Let's ask the lawyer," said the first Selectman.

Jim and the Mashpee folks watched the mails for the answer. On the day the letter came they were disappointed. The lawyer wrote that the court had said no. The Selectmen weren't discouraged. They asked again, this time getting all the important people they knew to ask with them.

Finally there was a meeting called for all Mashpee people. A Selectman stood up and announced:

"The court will let us use the extra money for our new school. With what the government will give us, too, there will be enough for a fine new building."

All the people cheered. When the clapping stopped, Jim stood up.

"I suggest we name the school for Mr. Davis," he said.

The townspeople agreed with a standing vote.

COOKIE GOES TO SEA

Joshua Taylor was seasick. The young boy hung over the rail of the Schooner Pennsylvania. He was so miserable he wondered why he ever wanted to be a sea captain. He was on his first voyage, starting as a cook as most young boys did. On this first short trip from Boston to Orleans he couldn't even stand up.

Some of the crew gathered around teasing him.

"This boy expects to sail to the Grand Banks and he can't make it to Boston and back," said one sailor.

"You're supposed to be our cook," said another. "Come on Cookie, get our dinner."

The mention of food made Joshua throw up. Why had he ever left his home in Orleans? Why had he ever agreed to cook for this awful crew? He'd be at sea with them for weeks. If he ever reached home, he'd never go to sea again.

Fortunately the mate, Samuel Sherman, came along and drove away the teasing men.

"Come on below deck and get in your hammock, Son," he said. "I'll cook dinner for you."

Mr. Sherman fed the hungry crew. He cleared up the dishes, leaving the galley shipshape. He also comforted Joshua with the news that the sea was calming. Soon the ship would be back in Orleans.

By late afternoon the Pennsylvania anchored at Billingsgate Island and Joshua was feeling much better. After being outfitted at Boston, the ship was to stay a few days in home port before heading out to sea. Joshua had time for a visit at home.

"I don't know if I want to be a sea captain or not," the boy told his parents. "I was awfully sick and those men were mean."

"They were just teasing," said his father. "You'll get used to them and the sea too. Besides, who will you pal around with at home? Every boy and man between 10 and 45 will be at sea this summer."

Joshua thought this over. Every one of his friends had already left on ships. Only the very young and the older men were left to work in the fields. Most of his friends were cooks. If they could do it he could too. Besides, he felt much better than he had that afternoon. Maybe it would be fun to go to sea.

"I promised. I'd better give it a try," he said.

The Pennsylvania made a stop at Provincetown to pick up fifty barrels of water and a load of firewood. Then the boat sailed the 900 miles to the fishing place in the Grand Banks.

Joshua's first breakfast was not a success. His coffee was too weak and he didn't make enough biscuits. Those he did make were tough. He had to eat hard bread himself.

"Let's tie these biscuits on the anchor chain," said a fisherman. "They're heavy enough to steady the ship."

"This coffee is like dishwater," said another. "Why not dump it overboard."

Joshua had a hard time holding back the tears. He should have stayed home. He didn't want to be a sea captain if he had to go through this.

Toward evening of the seventh day out from Cape Cod, the Captain took soundings with his lead and line. As soon as the lead struck bottom there was a bite.

"Let go the anchor. We're right on top of them," the Captain shouted. Soon two sailors hauled in a fine pair of codfish weighing ten pounds each. The sail came down. The anchor went out.

The next morning Joshua was up at 2:30 to get breakfast. He started the fire, then made biscuits and two gallons of coffee. Having been a cook for a week he had learned to make plenty. Everything was ready at 3:45 when the crew tumbled out ready for the day's fishing. There were no complaints about the food.

Joshua washed up the dishes quickly. He used sea water. Usually he polished them afterwards with wood ashes, but there was no time today. The boy went upstairs to watch the crew.

Five men manned the lines at a time. Each took care of two lines which had two hooks apiece. The men hauled in the fish as fast as they could, dumping them in their own deck boxes. After two hours the shift changed. Five more men took the lines. Now the fish in each box were counted and credited to the men. Then the catch was dumped into a large bin. Now it was Joshua's turn to work. He stood at the opening of the hold. After the men cleaned and washed the fish, Joshua threw them down the hold to the "salter". This man salted them and stored the fish away in barrels. Joshua's arm grew tired as this went on through the day. Everyone was glad when lunch time came.

By night time Joshua smelled of fish from head to foot.

The men joked with Joshua.

"For a little fellow he has a mighty good throwing arm," said one.

"It's a good thing he doesn't throw his biscuits," joshed another.

Now Joshua only smiled at their teasing.

That night the Captain wrote in his log the number of fish each man had caught. Joshua was glad to hear his friend Mr. Sherman had pulled in the most. He was the "highliner". All the fishermen together had caught 1800 fish. This was wonderful for the first day. It was a good crew. A Captain's job might not be bad after all.

The boy continued to like life on the schooner. He did get tired, but he was never seasick again. The hold grew full of fish barrels. "I wonder if I'll ever be able to scrub off the fish smell," he thought.

In between the hours spent pitching fish, Joshua became a good cook. Sunday was especially busy for him. The men rested, but the cook had to make doughnuts, apple duff and fried mince pies. Mr. Sherman came to his aid. It was good to smell something besides fish. The men liked Joshua's meals. "It isn't like Mother's, though," they joked. By this time Joshua understood their teasing.

One day two sails were sighted. Joshua rushed to the rail to watch the ships come closer. A great shout went up as the men recognized the Lapwing and the Stromboly from Orleans. The Captains came aboard to visit while the crew called across the water to their friends. The other Captains were surprised to find the Pennsylvania had its hold half full of fish. They had 40,000 pounds. Neither of the visiting schooners had caught more than 10,000 pounds.

Weeks later Joshua was home again, getting ready for the Captain's thank you dinner. The ship was unloaded. The salt fish had been doused in the ocean at high tide, then put on racks to dry in the sun.

Joshua pulled on his cleaned fisherman's clothing and walked toward the Captain's house. The stacks of codfish piled around the house looked like cord wood.

There was so much fish in the yard there was only a narrow path left to the door.

Joshua joined the rest of the men at the long tables that were spread with homespun cloth. His mouth watered as he looked at the deep dish chicken pie, the mashed potatoes and turnips, the browned gravy and the cranberry sauce. For dessert there were pies and fruit cakes.

The men ate heartily, for the women were good cooks.

"Nice to have a change from Cookie's food," chafed the men, "but I guess we'll sign him on for the next trip." Joshua grinned. The men wanted him back again!

After dessert was finished the Captain rose.

"Men," he said, "I've just had word from Boston. Our schooner broke the record, catching more fish this year than any other ship."

When the cheering died he added, "Our Sam Sherman was highliner for the whole fleet."

While the cheering made the roof resound and Joshua's ears ache, the boy decided, "It's a life at sea for me."

LITTLE LOST PILGRIM

One sunny day in July 1621 young John Billington wandered down an Indian trail near Plymouth. He turned into another trail that criss-crossed the first. He saw a perky chickadee and followed it down a third trail. Yellow flowers nodded to him so he turned down a fourth. Suddenly the way looked strange. John stopped. Which way was home?

The boy walked on intently looking for a trail he knew. Finally, tired, hungry and scared, he stopped again. "Pilgrims don't cry," he said to himself, so he trudged on over the criss-crossing paths. When it was dark, John lay down on the bank of a stream. In spite of the scary night sounds, he fell asleep.

Warm light shining on his eyelids woke him. Blueberries from a nearby bush were enough for breakfast. Then John started off again to find the way home.

Several days later, tired and bedraggled, John stumbled into a clearing. Three Indians sat around a fire. The red-skinned men looked up in surprise at this boy with the white skin.

"Squanto talks our language," thought John as he stared at the Indians. "Maybe they'll be friendly, too." The boy smiled shyly and called, "Hello! I'm hungry".

The Indians stared with puzzled looks. They did not answer. John made eating motions with his hands. Then the nearest Indian started toward him, holding out his bowl. John ate hungrily as the Indians crowded around him. They touched his face and hands. They felt his clothes. They did it so gently John wasn't afraid.

When the boy finished eating, the Indians motioned for him to follow them. For three days the Indians led John through the woods. Now and then he could see the ocean sparkling through the trees. The Indians were always kind, but many times the boy bit his lip to stop the tears. Nothing looked like the trails around Plymouth. Finally in desperation he turned to the Indians who had given him food.

"Where are you taking me?" he cried. The Indian stared at him, puzzled, then grunted and pointed ahead. John followed him sadly. "I'll never see home again," he thought.

At last John and the Indians came into a clearing where there were many Indians. They crowded around the boy in excitement. John was a little afraid, but he stood quietly while the natives touched his skin and fingered his clothing. Then his Indian friend took his hand, leading him to a very tall Indian draped in ornaments.

"This must be the Sachem," thought John. The Sachem listened to the Indians then turned to John. Lifting off one of his necklaces he placed it around the boy's neck. The Sachem patted John's shoulder.

A young Indian burst from the woods and ran to the Sachem. He spoke loudly, pointing at John.

"He must bring news about me," thought John eagerly. "Maybe the Governor is trying to find me." The runner finished and turned back into the woods. John watched hopefully.

Several days passed. Each morning more Indians came to see the white boy. John counted over a hundred natives camped around the clearing. Nothing happened, though, to show the Pilgrims were near. John kept hoping. He tried not to think of home so he wouldn't cry.

As John was eating supper that night, he glanced up from his food and gave a great shout. Squanto was walking toward him.

"Squanto, Squanto, take me home," John cried as he ran to the smiling Indian.

"I will," said Squanto. "Your people are near. You walked far to be at Nauset. First I will speak to Sachem Aspinet."

The Indians made a long line through the woods as they followed Aspinet and Squanto down the trail. John clutched Squanto's hand as if he'd never let go. He listened to the strange sounds of Indian talk around him. The trail led out of the woods onto sand dunes. The natives called and pointed as they saw a boat waiting in the shallow water.

"It's the pilgrim shallop," called John as he waved eagerly. "There's Captain Standish." The Pilgrims waved back.

"Up," said Squanto. John's Indian friend lifted him onto his shoulders and waded into the water. Half of the Indians waded with him toward the boat. The other half waited on shore, hands resting on their bows and arrows.

The Pilgrims reached for John, helping him over the side of the boat.

"Are you all right, boy?" asked Captain Standish.

"O yes. I'm fine, but am I glad to see you!" answered John.

"We'll thank the Indians with some presents," said Captain Standish, handing John's Indian friend a knife. "Here's one for Sachem Aspinet."

Then Captain Standish turned to Squanto who had climbed into the shallop.

"Please say thanks to Aspinet and his tribe," said the Captain.

Squanto spoke a few Indian words in a loud voice. The Pilgrims lifted their oars. John waved goodby. He could hardly wait to be home.

BENJAMIN HAS AN IDEA

Benjamin Dodd stared at the ship Nina, which lay half in and half out of the Provincetown post office. The vessel was tipped on its side with the bow thrust into the splintered roof. The stern rested on the sand outside. The tide had deposited the ship on top of the building, which had collapsed like an egg shell.

An excited crowd was gathered around, telling stories of yesterday's tidal wave.

"I never saw such a monstrous tide," said Benjamin's father.

"The damage is terrible all over town," said Schoolmaster Collins. "Some of the houses near shore were washed into the sea."

"First we'll help the folks who lost their homes," said Mr. Dodd. "Then we'll have to build a new post office. This one is a complete wreck."

"There's not enough lumber in town," replied the schoolmaster. "Too bad those houses on Long Point are so far away. We could use the empty ones here. The old schoolhouse would make a fine post office."

"Why can't you move them here?" asked Benjamin. It seemed to him Provincetowners were always moving houses around to suit the changes in their families.

"Too many sand dunes along the way," answered the school master.

The Town Crier's bell suddenly echoed down the street. "Hear ye, Hear ye," called the crier. "Mail will be at the general store tonight and every night until there is

47

a new post office. "Hear ye, Hear ye." His voice faded as the news was cried down the front and up the back streets.

Next morning Benjamin scuffed his way to the Center School. On his shoulder was a log of wood. When he wanted to, he could walk on the drifting sand so that not a grain got into his shoes. Or he could use the plank sidewalk, which so many townsfolks scorned because it had cost so much. This morning he was disappointed because school was in session, and so he scuffed. He had hoped to have another day at the harbor.

"Here's my log for today," said Benjamin to Mr. Collins as he came into the schoolhouse and dropped the log into the wood box. Each family paid part of the school costs in firewood and the boys carried a piece of wood to school each day.

Benjamin's mind wasn't on school. He was thinking about new houses and a new post office.

"Mr. Collins," he said. "I've been thinking about those houses on Long Point. Couldn't the men float them across the water, if they can't move them over land?"

"We've thought of that," replied the Schoolmaster. "But we don't have a barge big enough."

Rather shyly Benjamin said "How about making rafts out of wrecking barrels?"

The Schoolmaster stared at him thoughtfully.

"Benjamin, you might have something there. If wrecking barrels can bring up a vessel weighing many tons from the bottom of the sea, they ought to support a house," the Schoolmaster said. "I'll talk to the men tonight."

Next Saturday Benjamin hopped out of bed at dawn. He was so excited he couldn't sleep any longer. Today the men were going to try attaching wrecking barrels to one of the Long Point houses to see if it would float. He couldn't miss this.

Benjamin and his father had pancakes for breakfast, then left for the harbor. The boy helped his father, the Schoolmaster and the other men lash together a large number of barrels. These were attached to Benjamin's father's boat, then towed out to Long Point. They were anchored at the waters edge as the tide slowly went out.

Now the men must move the nearest empty house from its foundations up onto the makeshift barrel raft.

Ropes were attached and planks laid to make a temporary gang plank. Benjamin helped as the men pulled together mightily. Slowly the house moved over rolling logs up the gang plank and onto the raft. Now it was low tide. When the tide came in again, it would take only a little effort to float the raft loose. The men had lunch and a rest while they waited.

Soon the water was deep around the barrels. Benjamin helped the townsmen tug at the ropes.

"Hooray, it worked," called Benjamin to the Schoolmaster, as the raft floated on the water.

"This small house is floating fine," replied the Schoolmaster. "But I'm not sure if the school house will. We'll have to use a great many barrels. That's a large building."

That week several small houses were ferried across the bay. They became homes for those who had lost theirs in the storm. Now only two houses were left on the point besides the schoolhouse. The Lancys and the Cooks lived in them. These families had been lonesome way out on the Point away from the rest of the town.

"If empty houses can sail across the bay, full ones can too," declared Mrs. Lancy to her husband. "Let's move to town."

Mrs. Cook wanted to go, too, so it was agreed that the Lancy and the Cook houses would be carried across the bay. If the schoolhouse floated, that would come too.

An older man said bad weather was on the way. Others agreed, saying the moving project had better be finished in the next two days. So the men worked hard getting the houses on the rafts of barrels.

"Tomorrow will be a big day in Provincetown," thought Benjamin as he walked home from school on the sandy street. Suddenly he stopped.

"That's news for the Town Crier," he said aloud. Quickly he jumped up on the board sidewalk. He'd use the walks if they saved time. He ran toward the store, where the Crier's notices were left. The Town Crier was just approaching. Quickly Benjamin added his notice to the others on the slate.

Then the town crier was off ringing his bell and saying, "Hear ye, Hear ye. Tomorrow afternoon two homes and a schoolhouse will sail across the Bay. Hear ye! Hear ye!"

After school the next day there was a large crowd at the dock. Benjamin, his schoolmaster and all the pupils were at the water's edge. The people looked eagerly across the sparkling sea. Soon two houses were sighted.

"Why there's someone looking out the window of the Lancy's house," said one woman.

"Look, all the Cooks are in theirs," cried another.

"I can even hear their dog barking," shouted Benjamin. "They brought their pet for a sail." The crowd laughed with delight.

"No reason to walk as I could see it," said Mrs. Lancy as she stepped out of her house after its barrel raft had touched shore. "If the house was coming we might as well ride along."

50

"I have my supper cooking," said Mrs. Cook as she docked. "I notice people always have their appetites no matter what they're doing."

People were so interested in the docking of the houses and the remarks of the two ladies, they hadn't looked across the bay.

Then Benjamin shouted, "Mr. Collins, I see the schoolhouse coming. It floated! It floated!" He danced around in excitement.

"Wonderful, my boy," said Mr. Collins. "Because you used your head, Provincetown will have a new Post Office."

THE TOWN THAT BECAME FAMOUS

Little James Jarves peered eagerly over the rail of the ship "Polly" as it sailed toward Sandwich. The schooner was bringing little Jim and his parents from Boston to see his father's new glassworks. Jim watched the shoreline carefully, hoping to see the cone-shaped factory tower above the trees, remembering his father's description last winter.

"We're erecting a big building with a cone," his father had said. "Sandwich is a wonderful place for a glass factory for it has lots of sand and wood. It's near the ocean where the ships can land. You'll see it this summer, Son."

When Jim had told his friends at school they weren't very interested.

"I never heard of Sandwich," said one. "Where is it?"

"Nobody makes glass around here," said another.

Jim finally gave up. When school closed he just told them he was going away from the city for the summer.

A cloud of smoke was billowing up on the horizon.

"That's the glass works, Son," said Jim's father, coming to the ship's rail. "Look closely. You can just make out a tower in the smoke. That is where the bell hangs."

"What do you need a bell for?" asked Jim, who didn't see what that had to do with glass. His father laughed.

"The factory has many workers who work in shifts. The bell lets the village know when the shifts begin and end," he said

The Polly slowed down to moor at the dock. Jim noticed a crowd beginning to gather. Men, women, boys and girls jostled for places near the gangplank as Jim and his parents came down. Behind them came deck hands carrying packages and barrels. The Polly was a packet boat that carried people, mail and supplies from Boston to Cape towns.

Jim walked slowly, watching the people and the buildings in his new summer home town. As he climbed into the waiting wagon he said, "This place is not like Boston."

His mother pulled him to the seat beside her as the wagon started. "Our house is a grand one back home. Here it won't be as fancy," she said. "But you'll like it just as well. Remember, Sandwich is not a city like Boston."

Jim looked at the rolling dunes, the dirt road and the forest. That night as he climbed into bed in his new house he said, "I can hardly wait for morning to explore. I'm sure I'll find some real adventure."

"You can start with the glass works," answered his father, "if you get up early enough."

Jim climbed out of bed the first time his mother called and dressed hurriedly. After breakfast he followed his father down the path to the huge factory. It was warm inside. Men were throwing chunks of wood into an enormous fire. Large pots hung over the fire in which was molten glass.

"Today is a big day," said his father. "The foreman tells me they have the right mix. The glass is ready for blowing."

Several tall big-chested men stood near the fire holding long pipes.

"Those are the glass blowers I brought over from Europe, Jim," said his father. "It cost a lot, but I had to do it. No one on Cape Cod knew how to blow the glass."

"How did they learn?" asked Jim.

"Across the ocean it's a family trade," explained his father. "Each man teaches his son. These men learned from their fathers. Over here though, they'll have to teach Cape Cod men. Glass blowing is very difficult."

"It's a good thing they have big lungs for plenty of air," said Jim, looking at them closely.

"I imagine they developed that as they learned their trade," said his father. "Come along and meet them."

Suddenly the man watching the fires signaled. A helper lifted out a large glob of gooey glass from the pot. He gave it to the first blower who hooked it onto the end of his pipe. Jim watched in fascination as the blower swirled it round and round, blowing steadily. The glass grew like a balloon. Then a second blower picked it onto his pipe and blew and swirled while the first one got his breath back. Finally the head blower hooked it onto his pipe and formed a drinking glass.

"Now you can see why glassblowers have strong backs, fireproof skins and lungs like leather," laughed his father watching his son's amazed expression. "Come, let's look at the glass."

"Mr. Jarves, it's not too good," said the head blower. "It's not clear, and listen — it doesn't ring." The blower tapped the glass with his finger.

"What is wrong?" asked Jim's father.

"I think it's the sand," the blower answered.

"You mean, with all the sand on Cape Cod, I'm going to have to get some from some other place?" exclaimed Jim's father, with a frown.

Jim found other places to explore beside the glass factory. He climbed tall trees and found birds' nests. He roamed the seashore bringing home shells. He wandered down main street looking at the old houses, the mill and the church with the tall spire. He even slipped away to Mashpee to see the Indians. He was disappointed to see them dressed just like the people of Sandwich.

One night at supper Jim's father reported, "That sand I brought from New Jersey was what we needed. We're getting perfect glass and we can sell all we can make. The Polly's hold was almost full of glass today for the Boston market."

"Can I go see the blowers again tomorrow?" asked Jim. "I'd like to see what they make."

Next morning Jim watched the beautiful clear glass formed into many shapes by the blowers. Glasses, saucers, plates soon filled the shelves. Jim listened to the bell tones they made when tapped by the men.

A man came up to Mr. Jarves and held up a queer looking wood carving.

"Sir," he said,, "If we make a big mold like this and pour in glass, then put a smaller mold just like it inside, we could make glass without blowing."

Jim's father examined the object with growing excitement.

"You've got a good idea there," he said. "Keep working on it and we'll test it. Get the blacksmith to make a fireproof mold like your model."

Jim heard one glass blower snicker.

"Mr. Jarves won't really fall for that," he said. "Imagine making glass with a mold."

The day the mold was finished and ready to test Jim was there.

The workman brought out his mold and held it steady while another poured in the molten glass. Down went the plunger with the inner mold. It was fastened in place while the glass cooled.

No one went home. Even men from the early shift came to see the experiment. Finally the molds were removed. The crowd pushed forward, staring in amazement. The workman held a well formed decorated glass in his hand.

"Dishes and glasses can be made by a mold. We've got a new way to make glass. It will be cheaper too," cried Mr. Jarves. He was interupted by growls from the glass blowers. The crowd fell back to let them through. With a roar of anger the head blower cried,

"You're going to put us out of business with your molds."

Quickly Jim's father snatched Jim's hand and grabbed the glass. He rushed into the small office and shut the door. He sat down and wiped the sweat from his brow.

"I didn't think my first molded glass would cause a riot, Jim," he said. "But it is going to make big changes in the glass business."

"Are you going to get rid of the blowers?" asked Jim, looking anxiously at the closed door.

"No indeed," said his father. "But those men are too angry to talk right now. When they calm down I'll explain that we still need blowers for the fancy glass. This just means we can enlarge our factory and make molded glass for all the people who couldn't afford glass before."

The days passed all too quickly and soon Jim and his family were climbing aboard the Polly for the trip back to Boston.

"I wish I didn't have to go to school," grumbled Jim. "Then I could stay here in Sandwich."

"Some day you might be in charge of the factory," answered his father. "You'll need your schooling. Besides, you can look forward to coming back next summer."

Jim glanced down in the hold where barrels and barrels of molded and blown glass filled the hold.

"Our glass from Sandwich is famous now," said his father. "The labels on those barrels will take glass all over the country. Soon we'll be known in Europe too."

Jim smiled.

"The town is famous," he said. "Now I won't have to explain where I spend my summers."

WHALE IN THE BAY

Little Joe sat quietly beside his father in the old Truro church. It was town meeting and the men had gathered to settle town affairs. Joe was interested in the remarks of the men. Sometimes the voices sounded angry. Other times there was laughter. This didn't seem quite right in a church, but like most Cape churches, the building was used for meetings as well as services.

The voices went on. The patter of the rain on the roof and the steady drone of a long-winded speech made Joe sleepy. Now and then he would rouse when a drop of rain came through the roof. Once a drop spattered on his head and he moved over in the pew. The men were talking about money for a new church roof. Joe thought they had better stop talking and do something.

Suddenly young John Thatcher burst into the meeting house shouting "Whale in the Bay". At once the meeting ended. Everyone hurried toward the beach. Joe, no longer sleepy, ran after his father as fast as his shorter legs would carry him. He reached shore just in time to see boats being put into the water. The men of the town rowed out to the huge black object that was thrashing desperately in the shallow water of Cape Cod Bay. The boats drew close to the whale and the men killed it with their knives and boat spears. When the great whale was still, the men fastened lines to the spears and around the whale's body. Then it was towed slowly to the shore. The rain was stopping now and Joe looked intently as the body approached. He had never seen a whale close to.

The boy watched as the men on shore waded out to help drag the huge body onto the sand. At first everyone gathered around to see the long black whale with the blow hole in its head, then they went to work. There was wood to be gathered and fires to be built. Joe and the other little boys were sent to their homes for iron pots. Meanwhile some of the men had stripped off the fat, called blubber, with their knives. These men who had been to sea on whaling ships knew just how to do it. As soon as the fire was built, the blubber was put into the iron pots to boil. This was how whale oil was made. People all over the country wanted whale oil to burn in their lamps.

"We're lucky it's a blackfish," said Joe's father as he dropped a chunk of blubber in a pot. Joe remembered that the blackfish was a small whale which had in its head a part called a "melon". This made especially good oil that sold for 60 dollars a gallon.

"Will there be enough money to fix the church roof?" asked Joe. "It looks likely," said his father. Joe hoped there would be more than enough, then the men could buy the bell that the townspeople wanted. Joe sat down to watch. There would be no more town meeting that day. The work on the whale had to be finished before it began to smell. It was lucky the rain had stopped.

Later that week Joe drove the cows to pasture on the bay shore. He sat down on a little hill in the warm sunshine while the cows grazed. The water was calm, with small waves breaking gently on the beach. The tide was beginning to go out. Joe thought of the excitement the great drift whale caused and of the holiday the whole town had while the people got the oil ready for market. Then Joe thought of Uncle Silas, who was off on a big ship chasing whales. He decided to go to sea and hunt whales when he grew up. That would be more fun than shooing a herd of cows to pasture.

Quickly he sat up, breaking off his daydreams. There was an object thrashing around on the flats. The tide was way out now and the water was very shallow. The cows were busy eating. They wouldn't stray away. Joe waded out into the sea.

When Joe was close to the splashing object, he saw a whale like the great drift whale, only much smaller.

"It's only a little one," thought Joe, "But it has oil. There is no one around to call. I must do something before it gets away."

The tide was about to turn, bringing deeper water around the whale. Joe grabbed it by the tail, hanging on tightly in spite of the frenzied wiggles and splashes. Once he almost lost it as his small hands had a hard time holding on to the slippery skin. Gradually he pulled it closer to shore. Finally the whale stopped moving which made it easier. When the small whale was on the sand, he raced toward home shouting "Whale in the Bay".

Joe's father heard and came running, followed by the other townspeople. They were amazed that one small boy could wrestle in this little whale without any help. Again the boys ran for the pots and the townspeople gathered wood for the fires. The men started taking the blubber from the dead whale. Soon the oil was bubbling merrily in the pot.

"Good boy, son," said Joe's father. "You take after your Uncle Silas. When he was a boy he wrestled in a small whale too but it wasn't as big as yours."

Finally the oil was sold. There was enough money to buy a bell for the new meetinghouse. It would hang in the tower, above the newly shingled roof. Later Joe couldn't decide which was most exciting, catching the whale or tolling the bell.

THE LIGHT THAT MADE DAY LONGER

Tad rolled out of bed at his mother's call and jumped to the floor. Today was September 10th, the day Wellfleet families could begin picking bayberries. Tad pulled on his clothes quickly and climbed down the ladder from the loft.

"I'm glad Provincetown passed the law last year that no one could pick bayberries until a certain day," his father was saying as he motioned Tad to the table, "I'm sure that's how our town got the idea."

"Now we'll have a fair chance," said Tad, reaching for the mush. "Last year we didn't get enough bayberries."

Mother ladled out the cereal into bowls for Sarah and Jane, who were very quiet and still sleepy. "Wake up and eat, girls," she said. "We have to get started early. Last year remember, we ran out of bayberry candles."

Mother had already packed the lunches. Now she handed large baskets to the children as they finished eating.

"I hope we can fill these to the top," she said. "We need to get much more than this if we are going to make enough candles."

"Tad, you lead the way," said Father. "We'll start with the bayberries you discovered."

Soon the five were walking down the path to the sea. Tad skipped a few steps and swung his basket. Ahead the dunes, covered with beach grass, rolled gently down to the sea, sparkling in the early morning sunshine.

"This way," called Tad as he turned south along the shore.

After a long walk he pointed to a large grey-green patch of low bushes.

"What do you think of that?" he asked.

"Tad, you were right," said Mother. "This is the largest patch I have seen."

"Good work," said Father.

Sarah and Jane caught up with the others and all five knelt down by the low crooked branches. Cluster after cluster of the spicy small grey-green berries fell into the baskets. When anyone moved, the brittle branches snapped and cracked. Soon a delicious smell filled the air.

When all the baskets were filled, Tad put them under a tree and they all walked on to a patch Father knew. Later Father would collect all the baskets with the wagon.

"I'm tired of picking," said Jane as she sat down for lunch.

"We can't stop now," said Mother. "We have to keep picking until we have our winter supply. If we don't they will be picked by someone else."

"I'll tell you a story from my books," said Tad, "then you won't mind picking."

"Good idea," said Mother. "I wish we could get you more books. These you have are falling apart you read them over so much."

Jane and Sarah worked busily without any more complaints as Tad told story after story. When his voice grew tired he rested a bit then talked some more.

"We have to have more candles this year," he thought. "I need plenty of light to read and in winter it gets dark early."

Finally a week later, the shed was piled high with sweet smelling berries. Now it was time to start candle-making.

Tad and his father carried berry baskets into the house, piling them by the fireplace.

"I'm just like Benjamin Franklin today," said Tad. "He used to make candles with his family when he was little. It says so in the book Uncle Zenas gave me."

"I hope you'll be like Franklin when you grow up," said Father. "He was a wonderfully clever man".

Tad picked up a much-thumbed book from the table and opened it. "It says right here he helped his father make tallow candles when he was ten years old."

"You're better off than he was, Son," laughed his father. "Bayberries smell much better than tallow."

"There won't be any smell at all if some people don't get busy," said Mother briskly. "Let's get these berries cleaned and in the pot on the fire."

Soon the flames were leaping high on the hearth and one kettle was filled with melted berries. Another was put on the crane while the first was set on the hearth. It was Tad's job to skim off the oily wax mixture that gathered on top. This wax was put in a smaller kettle also at the edge of the fire. This kettleful had to be kept at just the right temperature for candle dipping.

Now Sarah and Jane went to work. They each held a stick from which dangled six cattails. These were dipped into the warm kettle of wax, then hung between two benches. More sticks with cattails from the swamp were made. As soon as one set was dipped, another was ready to be dipped again.

Tad had to be sure the wax stayed at just the right temperature. If it got too hot, the wax already on the candles would melt. Each time he moved the kettles Tad thought of the lovely light he would have to read by next winter, and somehow his arms didn't ache as much as before.

Finally the girls had made 36 dippings on all the candles. It was time to stop for the day.

"These are fine, girls," said Mother, looking the candles over carefully. "Tonight we'll pack some away in the attic."

At suppertime Father came in and handed Tad a package.

"Schoolmaster Crowell sent this package for you, Son," he said. "David Arnt was coming by on his horse and brought them."

"Books!" cried Tad, hugging the bundle whose cloth covering was partly off showing six big volumes.

"An old Parson in Chatham wanted them to go to a boy who loved to read. Schoolmaster thought of you," said his father, smiling at the boy's excitement.

After supper Tad carried his precious books and the new candles up the ladder to the loft. The books went by his bed. The candles went under the eaves. They were packed in a tin box to keep them safe from nibbling mice. One candle went by Tad's bed so he could read later on, when the sun went down. As he reached for the top book the green candles burning downstairs on the table sent the sweet smell of bayberry throughout the house.

THE GIRL WHO WENT TO SEA

Margery Baxter leaned against the rail of her father's ship, the JOHN N. CUSHING, and peered toward the horizon. Was that a sail? Perhaps it was a ship that would bring news of home, far away Cape Cod. Margery closed her eyes for a moment and imagined the square, white house with the Captain's walk which was back in Yarmouth, now half way around the world from here.

The little girl opened her eyes as a fish jumped out of water and splashed back. A large bird swooped down, too late to catch the fish. Watching the horizon again Margery thought, "I wouldn't like to see only water for 130 days like Phoebe Crowell."

A tantalizing smell came from the galley.

"I'm starved," said Margery, "and it isn't anywhere near dinner time."

With a last look across the empty sea, she jumped down the stairway two steps at a time.

Mother, Father and her older sisters Annie and Em were playing a game in the main cabin. Margery stepped around Rover, their big Newfoundland dog who always went with them to sea, and said to her father, "I'm so hungry. Can I have something from the munching drawer?"

"Why yes," said Father, drawing back his chair, "let's all have a little sweet."

Father went to the tall chest of drawers and opened the lowest section. As the children crowded around him Margery saw candies, nuts and even fruit, for they had recently been in port. The girls took a long time deciding. Margery finally chose a peppermint stick while her sisters took gum drops.

Suddenly there was a loud pounding at the door.

"Captain, come quickly," called the Mate. "The crew is fighting."

Captain Baxter ran out the door calling, "Lock the cabin after me and don't unlock it until I give the word. Keep Rover with you." Then he raced below deck.

"Is this a mutiny?" quavered Margery.

"I don't think so," said her mother, drawing her close, "but if it is your father will take care of it. Now help me bar the door."

When the door was locked and the girls had helped their mother roll the sea chest in front of it, Rover stretched out as if to say "Nobody will hurt you with me here."

Margery's mother settled her daughters on the bunk and distracted their attention with a story.

"You girls are not the only ones who have exciting times at sea," she said. "Let me tell you about a girl who went to sea by mistake. Her name was Spanish Teresa."

Margery, Em and Annie settled back against the cushions.

"One day in the far away country of Spain, a girl named Teresa went down to the harbor with her mother to sell flowers and fruit. They went aboard several ships and sold so much that Teresa had many coins jingling in her pocket. There were two ships left, so Teresa's mother divided the flowers. She took some to one ship while Teresa went to the other. As Teresa climbed the gangplank, she met the Captain's wife, Mrs. Parker, who bought all the flowers the little girl had. Teresa's pocket was heavy with coins. These would buy food for many days.

"Teresa had never been on quite such a large ship and she was curious. She stopped to watch the men loading the hold, then she wandered up to see the top deck. A big coil of rope made a lovely seat and she dropped down to rest a minute. Soon she fell asleep. She slept on as the great ship finished loading. She did not awaken as the gangplank was drawn in and the ship untied. As the ship set sail across the Bay she was still fast asleep.

"Early the next morning the mate discovered the little girl and brought her in tears to Mrs. Parker. Fortunately Mrs. Parker knew a few Spanish words and she was able to find out the girl's story. She shook her head sadly.

" 'Teresa, this ship has gone far from shore,' she said. 'It cannot turn back now. I'll help you write a letter to your mother to tell her where you are.'

" 'Don't worry,' she added kindly, 'You can stay with me on Cape Cod.'

"Teresa sailed to the new world and lived with the Parkers. She never did get back to Spain. When she grew older, she married a Mr. Cahoon of Hyannisport and had many children and grandchildren. Even though she lived to be 99, she never forgot her Spanish home and the mother she never saw again."

Margery sighed for Spanish Teresa, then angry shouts reminded her of the fight. The voices seemed nearer. Her mother looked anxiously around the room. Suddenly she rose and went to her piano. It was a wedding gift from the Mayor of Falmouth, England, Mother's home town. It went with Mother on all her travels. The carved oak wood and the silk panels gave the cabin a grand air.

Mother began playing and singing loudly. The girls joined her, singing song after song, until Captain Baxter's voice called. "Open up," he shouted, "All's well. The fighting has stopped."

The girls helped pull away the chest, then Mother unlocked the door. Rover barked a welcome as the girls hugged their father.

"Only a few black eyes and some bruised ribs," said Father. "Too much grog I guess. Now you girls will have another adventure to tell your children some day when you settle down on Cape Cod."

ABOUT THE AUTHOR

Marion Vuilleumier is a Cape resident, mother of three and wife of a clergyman. She has written extensively on Cape Cod history, is host of the television show Books and the World, and is executive secretary of the Cape Cod Writers' Conference.

Her books are: *The Way It Was on Olde Cape Cod, Indians on Olde Cape Cod, Sketches of Old Cape Cod, Craigville on Old Cape Cod, Churches on Cape Cod, Along the Wampanoag Trail, America's Religious Treasures, Cape Cod in Color, Martha's Vineyard in Color* and *Meditations By The Sea.*

ABOUT THE ILLUSTRATOR

Louis Edward Vuilleumier, son of Marion, is a graduate of Defiance College in Ohio with an art major. He is proprietor of the New England Art Gallery in Cummaquid which produces carved quarterboard signs and artistic antique slate gifts.